Original title:
Love and Friendship Through the Ages

Copyright © 2024 Swan Charm
All rights reserved.

Author: Sebastian Sarapuu
ISBN HARDBACK: 978-9916-86-728-0
ISBN PAPERBACK: 978-9916-86-729-7
ISBN EBOOK: 978-9916-86-730-3

Shelters Built from Affection

In warm embrace, we find our home,
A refuge from the world alone.
With whispered dreams, our hearts entwine,
In every glance, love's light will shine.

Together we craft a safe retreat,
With laughter and joy, our hearts repeat.
Each memory woven, strong and true,
In this shelter, it's me and you.

Bonds Beyond Boundaries

Across the miles, our spirits soar,
No distance can close the open door.
We share our dreams, our hopes and fears,
In every moment, love perseveres.

With every call, and every text,
A bond that time cannot affect.
Through ups and downs, we stand our ground,
In every heartbeat, love is found.

Kaleidoscope of Vibrant Moments

Life's colors dance in sweet delight,
In cherished times, hearts take flight.
Each vibrant hue tells a tale,
In laughter's echo, we prevail.

From sunrise's glow to moonlit nights,
In every shadow, joy ignites.
A tapestry of memories bright,
We weave our stories, bathed in light.

An Ode to Togetherness

In unity, we find our voice,
Together we celebrate our choice.
From whispered hopes to dreams declared,
In every heartbeat, love is shared.

With open hearts and hands held tight,
We face the world, embracing light.
In every moment, near or far,
Together, forever, that's who we are.

The Warmth of Shared Silences

In a room where whispers fade,
Quiet moments softly laid.
Hearts entwined, no need for words,
Echoed thoughts like song of birds.

Fingers brush, a knowing glance,
In stillness lies a gentle dance.
The warmth of souls, a gentle glow,
In shared silence, love can grow.

Even in the darkest night,
Silence wraps us, pure and bright.
Comfort found in hearts that beat,
In our stillness, life's complete.

Time drifts by without a sound,
In this peace, true love is found.
World outside fades far away,
Together here, we choose to stay.

These moments hold a magic rare,
In quietness, we lay our care.
Through every pause, in silence bound,
The warmest love is always found.

A Journey of Togetherness

With every step, we walk as one,
Underneath the same bright sun.
Hand in hand through trials faced,
In your smile, all fears erased.

Every turn unveils new sights,
Shared adventures fill our nights.
Dreams combined, we chart the course,
In your heart, I find my source.

Mountains high and rivers wide,
Together always, side by side.
Through the storms and sunlit days,
In our journey, love displays.

Every heartbeat sings our fate,
In our bond, we celebrate.
Two souls woven, strong and free,
In this journey, you and me.

Never lost, we navigate,
In your eyes, my true estate.
Guided by the stars above,
Our path unfolds, a tale of love.

Sunlit Paths

On paths aglow with golden light,
We wander freely, hearts in flight.
Through fields of dreams, by streams we roam,
In every step, we feel at home.

With laughter bright, the world unfolds,
Every moment, a tale retold.
Hand in hand beneath the sky,
As sunlit whispers pass us by.

The fragrant blooms, the gentle breeze,
Are mirrored in our hearts at ease.
Each day anew, our journey grows,
On sunlit paths, our love bestows.

Golden rays kiss every leaf,
In this warmth, we find relief.
Nature's canvas, vivid and bright,
Guiding us through day and night.

As evening falls, the stars emerge,
With every heartbeat, love will surge.
In sunlit paths, forever bound,
A sacred love in light is found.

Fusion of Hearts

Two souls collide, a spark ignites,
In this bond, love's purest flights.
Differences fade in the warmth we share,
A fusion of hearts, beyond compare.

Like rivers meeting, we intertwine,
In every glance, our spirits shine.
Together we're stronger than apart,
In the silence, we speak from the heart.

Moments crafted by fate's design,
Every laugh, every tear is divine.
With every heartbeat, rhythms blend,
In this dance, we're more than friends.

Through storms of life, we hold on tight,
In shadows cast, we find our light.
A tapestry woven, bright and bold,
In love's embrace, our story unfolds.

Hand in hand, we face each dawn,
In our fusion, we can't go wrong.
The world may change, but here we stand,
Together always, heart in hand.

Memories in Bloom

In the garden of our past,
Flowers whisper tales of old,
Sunset hues and shadows cast,
In petals soft, our dreams unfold.

Laughter dances in the air,
Fragrant scents of joy arise,
Moments cherished, beyond compare,
Captured in the twilight skies.

Hand in hand, we strolled along,
Time stood still in gentle grace,
Nature's chorus, our sweet song,
Each memory, a warm embrace.

Seasons change, yet still we find,
Roots of love that deeply grow,
In our hearts, forever kind,
A garden rich, where memories flow.

Heartstrings of Yesteryears

Tales we weave from days gone by,
Softly echo in the night,
Moments captured with a sigh,
Fading stars and silver light.

Every heartbeat tells a tale,
Of laughter shared, and tears we cried,
In the silence, love prevails,
Through the storm, we still abide.

Footsteps echo on the shore,
Waves of time crash at our feet,
In the distance, we explore,
Memories of the bittersweet.

Pages turning, life's rewards,
Golden threads through years embraced,
In our souls, forever stored,
Heartstrings tied, no love displaced.

Tides of Togetherness

In the ebb and flow of days,
We stand firm against the tide,
With every laugh, in countless ways,
Our hearts and souls are open wide.

Rising sun and glowing moon,
Guide us through the shifting sands,
Nature's dance, a timeless tune,
As we walk hand in hand in strands.

Storms may come, yet we remain,
Anchored deep in love's embrace,
Through the joy and through the pain,
Together, we find our place.

Whispers of the ocean's breeze,
Carry dreams into the night,
With each moment, hearts at peace,
Together, we shine so bright.

Timeless Connection

In a world where time can bend,
We find solace in each glance,
Through the years, our hearts transcend,
In a timeless, gentle dance.

Every laughter, every tear,
Threads that tie the fabric tight,
In our souls, you feel me near,
Guiding us through day and night.

Like the stars that grace the sky,
Constant in their glow and light,
Though we wander, you and I,
Always drawn, our spirits bright.

Moments shared, forever sewn,
In the quilt of life's embrace,
With each heartbeat, love is grown,
In our bond, we find our place.

Pages of Our Hearts

In whispers soft, our secrets lay,
Through ink and dreams, we find our way.
Each turn reveals a tender glance,
A dance of souls in sweet romance.

With every tear, a lesson learned,
In joy and pain, our hearts have burned.
We write our love on pages worn,
In histories of hope reborn.

The chapters bind, in twilight's hue,
Of timeless nights, just me and you.
With every word, our spirits soar,
A tapestry of evermore.

In laughter shared and silence deep,
We stitch together dreams we keep.
The story flows; it never parts,
In perfect sync, the pages start.

So write with me till stars align,
Each flick of pen, a love divine.
In pages worn, our truth imparts,
The endless tale of our great hearts.

The Ties That Time Weaves

In moments fleeting, threads unwind,
In hands we hold, our hearts combined.
The tapestry of life we trace,
In every smile, in every space.

With every tick, the clock chimes loud,
In whispered dreams, we feel so proud.
The ties that bind through vast expanse,
In seconds lost, we find our chance.

Through seasons change, we learn to grow,
In paths unmarked, we learn and flow.
Each memory a vibrant hue,
We paint our lives in shades so true.

Together still, as shadows cast,
In present moments, we hold fast.
The bonds we forge in laughter's light,
Stand strong amid the darkest night.

So let the winds of time embrace,
In every trial, we find our grace.
The ties we weave, a cherished sign,
In every heartbeat, intertwined.

Affectionate Chronicles

With gentle words, our stories start,
In precious notes, we share our heart.
Each line a hug, each word a kiss,
In soft reflections, we find bliss.

In every glance, a chapter waits,
With tender hands, we open gates.
The chronicles of laughter's spark,
Illuminate the paths we mark.

In shadows deep, or sunlight's glow,
Through every twist, our feelings flow.
The journeys penned, both far and wide,
With love as compass, we abide.

In fleeting moments, joy aligns,
As we etch memories in lines.
An affectionate script we share,
With every tale, we lay us bare.

So gather close, let stories weave,
In chronicle of hearts that believe.
With every voice, with every rhyme,
We write our love, transcending time.

Eternal Embrace

In twilight's glow, our shadows meet,
In softest whispers, love's heartbeat.
An eternal dance, two souls collide,
In every moment, love as guide.

The stars above, our witness stand,
In every touch, a gentle hand.
We weave a light that never wanes,
In every joy, in every pain.

Through tangled paths and winding roads,
Our hearts entwined, unburdened loads.
With every kiss, a brand new start,
In all we share, the truest art.

In silent nights, we dream and fly,
With love as wings, we touch the sky.
A promise made, we choose to stay,
In this eternal, wondrous play.

So hold me close, let time erase,
All fears and doubts in our embrace.
Together still, forever free,
In every breath, you live in me.

Reflections in the River of Time

Beneath the willow, shadows play,
Ripples whisper what we say.
Moments captured, hearts entwined,
In the flow, memories find.

Past and future, side by side,
In this stream, we must confide.
Ebbing gently, lessons learned,
In still waters, the heart yearns.

Waves of laughter, tears they hide,
Reflecting dreams, a timeless tide.
Every glance, a story told,
In the river, we grow bold.

Time won't linger, yet we strive,
To hold the moments, keep them alive.
In the current, we swim free,
Across the vast eternity.

In the dusk, as day takes flight,
We gather sparkles, pure and bright.
A chorus sung, a fleeting rhyme,
In the depths of the river of time.

Echoing Laughter in the Hall of Days

Soft echoes linger in the air,
Every moment, a love to share.
Footsteps dance on floors of light,
In the hall, our spirits bright.

Stories woven, tales unfold,
In laughter's warmth, we're consoled.
Each giggle, a thread divine,
Binding hearts, your hand in mine.

Walls adorned with memories sweet,
In every corner, joy's heartbeat.
Seasons change, yet we remain,
In this hall, love's quiet reign.

Time may fade, yet joy extends,
In each laugh, the past transcends.
A melody of days gone by,
In laughter's song, we learn to fly.

Together we rise, together we sing,
In every chuckle, a blossoming spring.
In the hall, our spirits sway,
Echoing laughter in the hall of days.

A Journey of Kindness

We tread the path with gentle hearts,
Every step, a work of art.
In the eyes of those we meet,
A journey blooms, kind and sweet.

Acts of love, small and grand,
Lifting spirits, hand in hand.
Through the storms, we learn to give,
In kindness, we truly live.

Words of hope, a gentle touch,
In the silence, it means so much.
Together we rise, in every prayer,
In the journey, kindness is our care.

Paths may twist, and shadows roam,
Yet in kindness, we find a home.
Together in laughter, in sorrow's embrace,
In this journey, we find our place.

Kindred spirits, our hearts align,
In simple gestures, love will shine.
A world reborn, in each new day,
In kindness, we find our way.

Chronicle of Cherished Souls

Pages turned, as time winds down,
In every story, a smile or frown.
Linked together by threads of fate,
Each soul's journey, resonate.

Through valleys deep and mountains tall,
In every rise, in every fall.
Wisdom gathered, tales retold,
In the chronicles, hearts unfold.

Moments captured, whispers shared,
In the tapestry, we are bared.
Every laugh, a tick of time,
In cherished bonds, we climb.

In shadows cast, we'll find the light,
Guiding souls through darkest nights.
A collection of love, in every scar,
In this chronicle, we are.

In every chapter, grace entwined,
In the pages, peace aligned.
A legacy of souls, we hold,
In this chronicle, our hearts bold.

Pathways of Connection

In shadows where the whispers weave,
Hearts entwined, we dare believe.
Through silence speaks a gentle tune,
Guiding us beneath the moon.

With every step, our souls ignite,
Illuminated by soft light.
We find our way through tangled fears,
Sharing laughter, drying tears.

The memories we craft from time,
Are threads that form a vibrant rhyme.
With every pulse, a bond we thread,
Together, where our dreams are led.

Through winding paths and rolling hills,
Our spirits dance, the heart fulfills.
In unity, we rise and sway,
Creating love in every ray.

So take my hand, we'll walk as one,
Beneath the stars, until we've spun.
A tapestry of joy and grace,
In pathways shared, our sacred space.

Roots and Blossoms

Beneath the earth, our roots extend,
A silent pact that will not bend.
In darkness, strength begins to grow,
As love and life begin to flow.

With every season, blooms arise,
A tapestry 'neath vibrant skies.
Petals soft and colors bright,
Reflect our journey, pure delight.

Through storms and sun, our branches sway,
Holding tight through night and day.
In every scar, resilience found,
Together, deeply soil-bound.

As shadows lengthen, stories swell,
In every leaf, a tale to tell.
From roots to blooms, we intertwine,
A sacred bond, forever divine.

With every breath, a pulse of green,
In nature's realm, our hearts convene.
Together, growing, wild and free,
In roots and blossoms, harmony.

A Bridge of Memories

Across the river, time flows wide,
Beneath its surface, dreams abide.
With every step on weathered stone,
We build a bridge to call our own.

The echoes of our laughter ring,
Each moment, a timeless swing.
Through every tale that we retrace,
Memories linger, interlace.

Connected by the threads we spun,
Each visit shared, a song begun.
In photographs, our smiles remain,
Fragments of joy, a sweet refrain.

As seasons shift and shadows play,
We gather moments, come what may.
In every glance, a spark ignites,
Sharing warmth on coldest nights.

The bridge we walk, a sacred span,
Unites our hearts, a perfect plan.
With every step, together roam,
In memories, we find our home.

Sagas of Two

In quiet corners, stories bloom,
Two hearts crafting a cozy room.
Through whispers soft and laughter light,
We weave our tales in starlit night.

Each chapter written, bound by trust,
In every dream, a shared gust.
The ink of love, it floods the page,
In moments fleeting, we engage.

Through valleys deep and mountains high,
We face the storm, together fly.
The strength of two, a force so grand,
A saga written, hand in hand.

With every tear, a lesson learned,
Through fire and grace, a passion burned.
In memories forged, we find our place,
Our journey, etched in time and space.

So here we stand, our spirits free,
In this vast world, just you and me.
With open hearts, let stories flow,
In sagas of love, forever grow.

Bridges Built on Shared Dreams

We stand on shores of hope,
With visions twinkling bright.
Two hearts, a common path,
Together, we ignite.

With laughter as our guide,
And trust as sturdy stone,
We weave our futures bold,
In unity, we've grown.

Each promise shared like gold,
A bond that will not break.
Through storms and sunny days,
We rise for love's own sake.

Hand in hand we march on,
With courage for the climb.
Our dreams become the bridge,
Transcending space and time.

Together we will shine,
With every step we take.
In the light of our shared dreams,
New worlds we will make.

Seasons of Togetherness

In spring, we plant the seeds,
Of laughter, hope, and care.
Through summer's warm embrace,
We find joy everywhere.

As autumn paints the leaves,
In hues of gold and fire,
We gather close and share,
The dreams that lift us higher.

When winter chills the air,
We huddle, hearts aglow.
In every season's turn,
Our love begins to grow.

Through cycles of our days,
We cherish what we find.
Each moment shared in time,
A tapestry entwined.

In every breath, a promise,
Together, side by side.
In seasons' swift embrace,
Our hearts forever tied.

The Warmth of Shared Silences

In quiet moments shared,
No need for words at all.
A glance, a gentle smile,
In silence, we enthrall.

The rhythm of our hearts,
A soft and soothing song.
Within this peaceful hush,
Is where we both belong.

Each whisper of the breeze,
Brings comfort, sweet and rare.
In stillness, we confide,
A world beyond compare.

With shadows drawing near,
We glow in twilight's grace.
In shared, unbroken time,
We find our secret place.

So let the silence speak,
As time drifts quietly by.
In warmth of shared moments,
Our spirits learn to fly.

Lanterns in the Shadows

When night falls silently,
With stars that faintly gleam,
We hold our lanterns close,
Together, we will dream.

The shadows may seem deep,
But hope lights up the way.
We walk through darkened paths,
With courage on display.

Each lantern glows with light,
A beacon strong and true.
In darkness, we find strength,
With every step we do.

As whispers rise like smoke,
We share our deepest fears.
In unity, we stand,
And conquer all our tears.

So let the night surround,
With dreams that softly spark.
Our lanterns shine so bright,
Together in the dark.

Whispers Across Time

In the stillness, voices call,
Through the ages, they enthrall.
Echoes linger, soft and bright,
Guiding hearts through endless night.

Memories dance on gentle shores,
As time unveils its hidden doors.
Every whisper, like a breeze,
Carrying love that never flees.

Silent messages in the stars,
Binding souls, no matter how far.
In the twilight, dreams take flight,
Whispers weaving, day to night.

Moments shared, yet far apart,
Time cannot break a loyal heart.
Each heartbeat sings a timeless tune,
A symphony beneath the moon.

In the echoes of what has been,
Lies the promise of what's unseen.
Through the ages, love remains,
Whispers carry through joys and pains.

Bonds Unbroken

In the fabric of our days,
We weave a bond that never sways.
Ties of love that hold us fast,
Anchored deep and built to last.

Through laughter shared and tears that fall,
Resilient through it all.
With every challenge that we face,
Our hearts entwined, we find our place.

From distant shores to close embrace,
Every meeting, a sacred space.
In silence, knowing looks exchanged,
In every moment, life re-arranged.

Hands held tight, as storms arise,
With steadfast trust, we reach for skies.
In the warmth of each other's gaze,
We find our strength, we find our ways.

No distance vast, no time too long,
A melody that sings our song.
In every heartbeat, love's a token,
In our souls, the bonds unbroken.

Echoes of Affection

In the silence, love's refrain,
Soft as whispers, sweet as rain.
Echoes linger, warm and near,
Each memory a treasure dear.

In laughter's glow and sorrow's sway,
Love's reflection leads the way.
Through every moment, joy and strife,
Echoes shape the dance of life.

Hand in hand through shifting sands,
Together we make our own commands.
With gentle words that bridge the years,
Our bond withstands both joy and fears.

In the softest touch, we find,
A whispered promise intertwined.
Echoes of the heart resound,
In every silence, love is found.

As shadows stretch and daylight fades,
We linger where our laughter wades.
Through the echoes and light reflections,
We celebrate our deep affections.

The Tapestry of Togetherness

Woven threads of bright and bold,
Stories shared and secrets told.
In the tapestry, colors blend,
A masterpiece that will not end.

Each moment stitched with care and grace,
In every corner, love's embrace.
Through challenges, we stand as one,
Creating patterns in the sun.

With laughter's hues and sorrow's stains,
The threads of life hold joys and pains.
In the fabric of our days combined,
Rich and deep, our lives aligned.

Together we face the winds of change,
In our bond, we can rearrange.
Through every twist and every turn,
In the tapestry, our hearts burn.

As we gather threads of dreams anew,
Together we craft a vision true.
In this tapestry, forever thine,
Hand in hand, our souls entwined.

Echoes of Affection

In shadows cast by fading light,
Laughter weaves through quiet nights.
Soft memories linger, then depart,
Echoes gently fill the heart.

With every sigh that softly speaks,
Time molds our paths, though it feels weak.
Yet love's embrace remains so clear,
In every moment, we hold dear.

Through whispers shared beneath the stars,
We paint our dreams, erase the scars.
In every hug, a safe retreat,
A dance of souls, so bittersweet.

As seasons change, we stand so tall,
Together facing every fall.
The world outside may drift away,
But here in love, we choose to stay.

Through echoes of sweet joy and pain,
Together we have much to gain.
In every heart, a story spun,
In quiet moments, love's begun.

Timeless Bonds in Twilight

In twilight's glow, we find our place,
Timeless bonds time can't erase.
Hand in hand, we gently sway,
Guided by love's eternal ray.

With every hour the sun descends,
Laughter flows, and joy transcends.
In tender glances, secrets share,
A promise made in whispered air.

As stars awaken in the night,
We gather dreams, prepare for flight.
From dusk till dawn, our spirits soar,
In unity, we seek and explore.

Old stories told by fire's warm glow,
Each word a thread in love's fine flow.
Through trials faced, together we stand,
In every footstep, hand in hand.

In every heartbeat, forged anew,
Timeless bonds forever true.
Through twilight's calm, our souls unite,
In love's embrace, we seek the light.

Whispers Across Generations

Beneath the oak, old stories rest,
Whispers soft, a loving jest.
Voices echo through the trees,
Guiding hearts like a gentle breeze.

From past to present, tales unfold,
In every smile, a thread of gold.
Lessons learned in laughter's grace,
Generations weave time's embrace.

With every hug that bridges years,
We share our hopes, we share our fears.
The strength of roots, the joy of flight,
Together we bask in shared light.

Through every sunset, hand in hand,
We cherish dreams, and make our stand.
The circle grows, the love expands,
In whispered tales, the heart understands.

Across the ages, bonds withstand,
In life's great book, we take our stand.
With whispered grace, we pass the flame,
Embracing love, we stay the same.

The Tapestry of Togetherness

In threads of time, our lives entwine,
A tapestry both bold and fine.
Each color bright, each shadow cast,
In unity, we hold steadfast.

Through every patch, a memory sewn,
In laughter's warmth, we've brightly grown.
With tears that mingle, joy takes flight,
Together we weather day and night.

The fabric rich with stories told,
From heart to heart, a bond of gold.
In every challenge, hand in hand,
We stitch our dreams, we make our stand.

As seasons turn, our love will weave,
A pattern strong, we won't deceive.
Through trials faced, we rise anew,
In every thread, our love shines through.

Together we create, we mend,
A tapestry that knows no end.
In every moment, dance and sing,
Together, we are everything.

A Mosaic of Shared Journeys

We travel paths both new and worn,
In every step, a story born.
Together through the sun and rain,
A tapestry of joy and pain.

With every laugh, a piece we share,
In silent moments, love laid bare.
Our memories like dots combine,
To paint a picture, rich and fine.

In winding roads, we find our way,
In gentle whispers, words convey.
Through valleys deep and mountains high,
Each journey made, we learn to fly.

The colors blend, the edges meet,
In unity, our hearts compete.
As we forge ahead, hand in hand,
A mosaic crafted, planned and grand.

In every turn, we grow and shift,
Each chapter read, our hearts uplift.
And when we pause, and look around,
In shared journeys, home is found.

Carved in the Stars

Beneath the vast celestial dome,
We search for signs, we make our home.
Each twinkling light, a tale untold,
Of dreams and hopes, both brave and bold.

With every night, we gaze and find,
A universe, both vast and kind.
In constellations, paths align,
A dance of fate, a grand design.

Through trials faced and battles fought,
In every star, a lesson taught.
We carve our names through time and space,
With every wish, we leave a trace.

The moonlit glow guides every heart,
In darkness deep, we play our part.
A luminous thread in love's embrace,
Together we weave our sacred space.

As eons pass and ages flow,
Our spirits rise, they shine and glow.
In this cosmic tale, we trust,
For love, like stars, is fair and just.

The Symphony of Shared Lives

In harmony, our voices blend,
A symphony that knows no end.
Each note we play, a story shared,
In every chord, we find we cared.

Through laughter's rush and sorrow's sigh,
Our melodies, they rise and fly.
In whispers soft and shouts so bold,
The music of our lives unfolds.

With every beat, our hearts align,
In rhythm found, our souls entwine.
From gentle strings to thunder's roll,
Together we compose our soul.

In every season, change we embrace,
The symphony, our saving grace.
In dissonance, we find our tune,
Our hearts beat on, beneath the moon.

As time's great score unfolds its page,
In quiet moments, we engage.
With love's refrain, life's dance we share,
A symphony that fills the air.

Chronicles in the Garden of Time

In gardens lush, where memories bloom,
We plant our hopes amid the gloom.
Each petal soft, a story told,
In whispers sweet, our dreams unfold.

The seasons change, yet we remain,
In sunlight's warmth and gentle rain.
With roots that dig into the past,
We shape our future, hold it fast.

Each flower's scent, a tale we weave,
Of laughter shared, of hearts that grieve.
In every leaf, a lesson learned,
In time's embrace, our spirits turned.

The trellis stands, our lives support,
In blooms of love, we find our fort.
With every dawn, new hopes arise,
In nature's arms, we find our ties.

As evening falls, we gather round,
The stories linger, deeply found.
In every moment, honored, prime,
We write our chronicles in time.

An Unfolding Story

Once upon a quiet night,
Whispers danced in silver light.
Pages turned with gentle grace,
Each word a soft embrace.

In shadows where dreams reside,
Tales of love and hope abide.
Through the ink, a journey flows,
As the heart forever knows.

With every sigh, a chapter's penned,
Fates entwined, there's no end.
Moments stretch like softest threads,
Binding souls in silent spreads.

Hands of time turn pages fast,
Memories from the past are cast.
In every line, a heartbeat's beat,
Life unfolds, both bittersweet.

So let us write, both you and I,
Underneath the starry sky.
As long as life's ink still flows,
Our story, forever grows.

Imprints on the Soul

Fingers trace the tales of old,
Every memory worth its gold.
Footprints left on sandy shores,
Carry whispers, fade, but soar.

In laughter shared, a bond is born,
Through silent tears, we are reborn.
The echoes of our past remain,
Carved like art through joy and pain.

Each heartbeat sings a timeless song,
Reminders of where we belong.
In stillness, find the truth we seek,
In every scar, our spirits speak.

With open hearts and seeking eyes,
We navigate the endless skies.
Imprints left will never fade,
In the love that we have made.

So treasure every moment dear,
For in those times, we feel you near.
A tapestry of grace unfurls,
As life's beauty whirls and twirls.

The Circle of Us

Within a ring, our laughter glows,
In every heart, a kindness flows.
Through ups and downs, we hold so tight,
Shining brightly, in darkest night.

The circle's strong, it bends but stays,
Embracing all in myriad ways.
In joyful leaps and quiet sighs,
Together we chase the boundless skies.

In every story, a thread connects,
Through shared dreams, life intersects.
Hand in hand, we find our way,
Guided by love, night or day.

From whispered hopes to shouts of cheer,
We weave a path that's crystal clear.
A circle formed with hearts so pure,
In each embrace, we feel secure.

So let this bond forever grow,
With every ebb and every flow.
Together we dream, together we trust,
In this forever, the circle of us.

Daisy Chains and Dusty Roads

A field of daisies, soft and bright,
We weave our dreams in golden light.
With laughter echoing on the breeze,
Each chain a bond, each flower a tease.

Footprints trailing on dusty roads,
Adventures shared, our hearts bestowed.
Through paths unseen, we roam so free,
In every turn, it's you and me.

The sun sets low, painting the sky,
With memories made as days go by.
Through tangled woods and open plains,
We dance and sing in joy, in pain.

Handcrafted tales from moments shared,
In daisy chains, our souls laid bare.
With every step, the road unwinds,
Connecting hearts, creating binds.

So let's wander, with dreams in hand,
Through fields of gold and shifting sand.
For daisy chains will guide us home,
No matter where our feet may roam.

The Essence of Togetherness

In laughter shared, our spirits soar,
With every hug, we heal the sore.
Hand in hand, we face the night,
Together we shine, a guiding light.

In silence shared, our hearts align,
In every moment, love we find.
Through trials faced, we stand so strong,
In unity, we all belong.

In every tear, a bond we weave,
With open hearts, we dare believe.
Beyond the storms, we rise and play,
Together always, come what may.

In joyous days, we lift each other,
Each whispered truth, a cherished tether.
With every step upon this ground,
In each embrace, our peace is found.

The essence lies in all we share,
In every story, every prayer.
Together, friends, we write our song,
The essence of us will always be strong.

From Youth to Wisdom

In youth we dance, so wild and free,
Each day a chance, our dreams to see.
With laughter loud, we chase the dawn,
In innocence, our fears are gone.

As seasons change, we learn and grow,
In every heart, a tale to show.
With wisdom gained, we find our role,
In every step, we touch the soul.

From fleeting time, we craft our fate,
In every choice, we contemplate.
With open eyes, we face the truth,
In every lesson, echoes of youth.

In quiet moments, we reflect,
On paths we've walked, the roads connect.
With every scar, a story shines,
From youth to wisdom, the journey binds.

The tapestry of life unspooled,
In every thread, the heart is fueled.
From dust to dreams, we take our stand,
In time's embrace, we understand.

A Lifetime of Echoes

In whispered words, the past does speak,
Echoes dance upon the peak.
Through gentle winds, the stories flow,
A symphony of all we know.

In every laugh, a memory clear,
In every sigh, love draws near.
With every year, our voices blend,
A lifetime's song that will not end.

Through valleys deep and mountains high,
In courage found, we learn to fly.
With every step, we hold the grace,
Of every heart we dare to face.

In shadows cast, we find the light,
In every wrong, the path to right.
With every echo, we stand tall,
In this lifetime, we give our all.

A journey shared, we walk as one,
Beneath the moon, beneath the sun.
In echoes grand, our spirits flow,
In love's embrace, we come to grow.

Gentle Reminders

In softest whispers, the world awakes,
Gentle nudges, a heart that breaks.
With morning sun, a new day calls,
In every smile, love never falls.

In peaceful moments, we find our way,
With calming breaths, we seize the day.
As storms may rage, and fears arise,
In gentle reminders, hope never dies.

In tender touches, the soul's embrace,
A quiet strength in every space.
With every glance, the heart responds,
In gentle nudges, our spirit bonds.

In golden leaves, the autumn's grace,
In every season, we find our place.
With every heartbeat, a truth we share,
In gentle reminders, we learn to care.

With every moment, a chance to grow,
In love's soft light, the truth we know.
Gentle reminders from heart to heart,
In unity's song, we play our part.

The Harmony of Us

In whispers soft, we find our tune,
Together under the silver moon.
A dance of dreams, where hearts align,
In every step, your hand in mine.

Through storms we weather, side by side,
In joy and sorrow, our hearts confide.
A symphony of laughs and sighs,
In the melody, love never dies.

With every note that fills the air,
A bond that deepens, pure and rare.
We mend the cracks, we bloom and grow,
In harmony, our spirits flow.

Like rivers run, our paths entwined,
In every heartbeat, love defined.
Through seasons change, we hold our place,
In perfect rhythm, in warm embrace.

From distant shores to valleys wide,
In every dream, your love my guide.
With open hearts, we face the day,
In harmony, we find our way.

Echoes of the Past

Upon the hills where shadows lay,
Whispers of times long gone, they play.
In memories etched like fading light,
We gather pieces of lost delight.

The laughter shared, the tears we cried,
In every moment, our hearts abide.
Through echoes soft, the past we greet,
In every heartbeat, we feel the beat.

The stories told beneath the stars,
Remind us all of how we are.
In pages worn, the truth we trace,
A tapestry of time, we embrace.

Though paths diverge and seasons wane,
The bond remains, through joy and pain.
In every echo, a lesson learned,
The flame of love forever burned.

As future calls, we turn around,
In every heartbeat, love is found.
From yesteryears, we draw our strength,
In echoes deep, we find our length.

Mosaics of Togetherness

Pieces scattered, colors bright,
In every shard, a gleam of light.
Together crafting, hand in hand,
A vibrant world, a promised land.

In laughter's echo, a joyous sound,
In every corner, love is found.
With gentle hands, we build and weave,
A mosaic rich, we dare believe.

Through trials faced and storms we brave,
Each broken piece, a path we pave.
In unity, our hearts ignite,
The bond of love, so pure and right.

With dreams that soar on wings of hope,
In every struggle, a way to cope.
Each moment shared, a brushstroke cast,
Together forged, our shadows past.

In every hue, our stories blend,
A masterpiece that has no end.
In the gallery of life we meet,
Our hearts entwined, our lives complete.

The Dawn of Kinship

As morning light begins to break,
A world reborn, we softly wake.
With open arms, we greet the day,
In kinship's warmth, we find our way.

Through whispered dreams and shared delight,
In every heartbeat, love ignites.
With every dawn, new hopes we share,
A bond unspoken, pure and rare.

With every step on this shared ground,
In unity, our hopes are found.
Through trials faced, we rise anew,
Together strong, in hearts so true.

The sun ascends, its golden rays,
Illuminate our intertwined ways.
In every laugh, in every tear,
Our kinship grows, expanding near.

As bright horizons stretch so wide,
In the dawn's glow, we walk with pride.
With every heartbeat, we embrace,
The dawn of kinship, a sacred space.

A Symphony of Souls

In quiet whispers, hearts combine,
Strumming gently like rambling vines.
Melodies rising, tender and clear,
Each note a memory, drawing us near.

A dance of shadows beneath the stars,
Echoes of laughter, healing past scars.
Voices entwined in harmonious flow,
A symphony blooms where love dares to grow.

Together we wander, hand in hand,
Creating a story, both simple and grand.
The music of life, both sweet and profound,
A symphony of souls, forever unbound.

Through valleys of silence, the chords softly play,
Guiding our spirits along the way.
In every heart's beat, a voice intertwines,
Crafting a tale that eternally shines.

With every crescendo, the world holds its breath,
Each harmony sings of life and of death.
This tapestry woven, we cherish and hold,
A symphony timeless, more precious than gold.

Orange Blossoms and Old Letters

In the attic, where dust gathers thick,
Old letters whisper, their secrets a trick.
Orange blossoms breath memories sweet,
Of lovers long gone, and their bittersweet beat.

Fragments of love, stained with time's hand,
Stories of youth, like grains of sand.
Each penned word dances on fragile pages,
A romance alive, through the silent ages.

Beneath the sun, their fragrance takes flight,
Echoing laughter that vanished from sight.
Worn hands unfold tales of joy and of pain,
Orange memories blossom, like soft summer rain.

Together we linger, in this cherished space,
Finding solace amongst lace and grace.
A treasure trove holds what time can't erase,
Old letters and blossoms, a timeless embrace.

Revealing the past in fragrant delight,
Each petal a promise, each stroke a light.
In stillness we share this enchanted song,
Of orange blossoms and letters, where we belong.

Woven Through the Seasons

In the spring's blush, new life breaks free,
Colors awaken, a vibrant decree.
The earth spins softly, a quilt unfolds,
With stories of warmth that nature holds.

Summer beckons with sun-kissed days,
Laughing children in warm golden rays.
Fields painted bright in a playful spree,
Woven threads dance in our shared jubilee.

As autumn descends, the leaves turn bold,
A tapestry rich with crimson and gold.
Whispers of change flutter down from the trees,
Nature's embrace carries soft, gentle breezes.

Winter's chill brings a tranquil pause,
Where quiet reflections earn applause.
Under blankets of white, we dream and we sigh,
Each season's a chapter, a reason to fly.

Through cycles of life, our spirits unite,
Woven through seasons, a beautiful sight.
In each breath we take, both tender and true,
The fabric of time connects me and you.

Tethered by Time

In the grip of moments, we stand so close,
Tethered by time, like roots of a rose.
Each laugh and tear, a thread in our tale,
Binding us gently when love seems frail.

Through the years passed, memories do shine,
Creating a beacon, forever entwined.
The tick of the clock sings sweet lullabies,
Playing the music of our shared sighs.

Suspended in twilight, where dreams come alive,
Our hearts beat as one, we flourish and thrive.
The beauty of presence, in moments we find,
A tapestry woven, forever aligned.

As shadows grow long, and daylight will wane,
Together we weather both sorrow and gain.
With each whispered promise and cherished embrace,
Tethered by time in this sacred space.

In the quiet of night, as stars softly gleam,
We weave through the darkness, awakening dreams.
With every heartbeat, and every sigh,
Tethered by time, we learn how to fly.

The Dance of Devotion

In the light of the morning dew,
Hearts entwined, a love so true.
With every step, we weave our song,
In this dance, where we belong.

Through whispers soft and hands held tight,
Our spirits soar, taking flight.
With passion's fire, we gracefully sway,
In this dance, come what may.

The rhythm beats like a longing heart,
In perfect sync, we play our part.
With every glance, our souls ignite,
In this dance, love feels so right.

As twilight glows, we spin and turn,
In this embrace, our hearts will learn.
With every pirouette, we celebrate,
In this dance, we cultivate.

In the silence where moments meet,
A promise held, no need for defeat.
With grace we move, shedding fears,
In this dance, through all the years.

Stars Aligned

Under a canvas of midnight blue,
The stars gather, painting for you.
Whispers of dreams in the cosmic light,
In this moment, everything feels right.

With galaxies spinning in celestial grace,
We find our place in this vast space.
Fate's fingers trace our paths with care,
In this dance, we sense the air.

As constellations guide our way,
We walk this path, come what may.
With every heartbeat, the universe sighs,
In this dance, our destiny lies.

The moon gazes, a watchful eye,
As time flows like the night sky.
With hope we wish upon a star,
In this dance, we know who we are.

Together we shine, brilliant and bright,
Two souls merging in guided light.
As the cosmos sings and aligns our fate,
In this dance, we celebrate.

Seasons of Us

In spring's embrace, our dreams take flight,
Petals blooming, hearts so light.
With every laugh, the world awakens,
In this season, love's unshaken.

As summer sizzles, days grow long,
In golden light, we hum our song.
With sun-kissed smiles, we chase the breeze,
In this season, our hearts find ease.

Autumn whispers, leaves will fall,
In hues of amber, we hear the call.
With cozy nights and fireside chats,
In this season, togetherness wraps.

Winter blankets us in soft white snow,
As the world quiets, love starts to glow.
With warmth inside, we hold each other,
In this season, we are no other.

Through changing tides, our journey flows,
In every season, our love grows.
With every turn, we'll endure the fuss,
In this dance, it's always us.

Reflections of Kinship

In mirrored glass, our stories dwell,
Shared whispers of joy and tales to tell.
With roots entwined, we stand as one,
In this bond, the journey has begun.

Through laughter's echo, we find our strength,
In every hardship, we go to great lengths.
With arms wide open, we embrace the past,
In this reflection, love will last.

From childhood dreams to grown-up fears,
We navigate life through smiles and tears.
With every challenge, we stand side by side,
In this kinship, we abide.

With stories woven in a vibrant thread,
In moments shared, the words are said.
With hearts so warm, we cherish the tale,
In this reflection, we will prevail.

As seasons change, and paths may shift,
In every heartbeat, our spirits lift.
With bonds of love, we'll forever be,
In this dance, just you and me.

The Map of Us

In every turn, our paths entwine,
With footprints traced in sands of time.
Mountains climbed and rivers crossed,
Each landmark speaks of love embossed.

Through storms we sailed, not lost at sea,
Your heart, a compass guiding me.
We chart our dreams both near and far,
Forever drawn, our guiding star.

With every journey, tales we tell,
In whispered winds, where spirits dwell.
Together we roam, side by side,
This map of us, our hearts abide.

We sketch our hopes in colors bright,
In shadows deep, we find our light.
Together laughter, joy, and tears,
A map of us through all the years.

With threads of fate, our story's spun,
In this vast world, we've just begun.
Each mile a memory we will share,
The map of us, beyond compare.

Sculpted by Emotions

In the stone of silence, we find our grace,
Chiseling moments in this sacred space.
With hands of tenderness, we carve our bond,
Sculpted by emotions, our hearts respond.

Each tear a drop to shape our art,
In laughter's echo, you've touched my heart.
Together we mold, both joy and strife,
Crafting a masterpiece, this is our life.

In clay of compassion, our forms unite,
Reshaping shadows into light.
We sculpt our dreams, both fierce and bold,
In every curl, our tale unfolds.

In every heartbeat, a new design,
Chiseled by moments, so divine.
With love as our chisel, faith as our mold,
A sculpture of hearts, our treasure untold.

Through storms and sunlight, we find our way,
Sculpted by emotions, come what may.
In the gallery of us, forever displayed,
Artisans of life, with love, we've made.

A Canvas of Companions

In hues of laughter, our colors blend,
Strokes of friendship, on you I depend.
A canvas alive, with stories bright,
Together we paint, both day and night.

Each splash of joy, a moment shared,
In trials faced, how much we dared.
With every brush, our souls aligned,
In this masterpiece, our hearts entwined.

We layer our dreams, both fierce and free,
In the gallery of hearts, just you and me.
In shadows cast, we find the light,
A canvas of companions, pure delight.

With vibrant hues, we greet the dawn,
In the art of life, we've sworn to bond.
Brush strokes of love, both tender and bold,
On this canvas, our story's told.

Through seasons changing, colors shift,
In every layer, our spirits lift.
A canvas of companions, we've made our mark,
In the heart of art, forever a spark.

The Pulse of Togetherness

In rhythm of life, our hearts align,
With every beat, our souls combine.
The pulse of togetherness, strong and clear,
In every moment, love draws near.

Through silence shared, a song we sing,
In whispers soft, our spirits cling.
Together we dance, in life's embrace,
The pulse of togetherness, a sacred space.

With laughter ringing, like bells in tune,
We celebrate under the silver moon.
In the tapestry woven, our threads shine bright,
The pulse of togetherness, day and night.

In storms we gather, steadfast and true,
With every heartbeat, I stand with you.
A bond unbroken, we rise and fall,
The pulse of togetherness, our all in all.

In every heartbeat's echo, love remains,
In the dance of life, joy intertwains.
Fulfilling stories, we both adorn,
The pulse of togetherness, forever reborn.

The Language of Laughter

In a room filled with cheer,
Laughter cascades like rain.
It dances from lips so near,
 Washing away all pain.

Joy is woven in the air,
Connecting souls with glee.
A universal prayer,
Where hearts can truly see.

Every chuckle, every grin,
 Unites us in a song.
Where kindness can begin,
And we feel we belong.

Echoes of joy resound,
In memories we share.
In laughter, we are found,
Binding hearts with care.

Let jokes be the fine thread,
Stitching hope in our dreams.
In every smile widespread,
 The light forever beams.

Threads of Connection

In the tapestry of life,
Threads intertwine and weave.
Binding us through joy and strife,
In every story we believe.

A glance can spark a fire,
A touch can heal the heart.
In whispers, we conspire,
Each moment plays its part.

Paths cross in random ways,
Like stars that fill the night.
These connections gently blaze,
Illuminating our sight.

Each bond is a gentle thread,
Stitched in the fabric of time.
Through laughter, love, and dread,
We find our rhythm, our rhyme.

In shadows, we are linked,
Even when apart we stand.
Through every word, we've inked,
A unity so grand.

As threads of gold do shine,
In every heart they're spun.
In life's grand design,
Together, we are one.

Embracing Moments Lost and Found

In the silence of the past,
Whispers echo through the air.
Moments fade, but love holds fast,
In memories, we are aware.

Each heartbeat tells a tale,
Of laughter, tears, and grace.
Through storms, we will prevail,
Finding warmth in each embrace.

Shadows linger in the light,
Beauty rests in what we've shared.
In lost dreams, we find our sight,
In the moments we have dared.

Time may steal what we hold dear,
Yet within, it's still profound.
In every smile and tear,
We grow closer, hearts unbound.

So take a breath, and feel it near,
Embrace the waves that come and go.
For in the depths, there's nothing to fear,
As love remains in every flow.

Lost and found in life's embrace,
We're woven threads of fate.
In every moment, we find grace,
Together, we create.

Starlit Promises

Underneath a velvet sky,
Stars twinkle with a spark.
Each one a wish held high,
Guiding dreams out of the dark.

In the silence of the night,
Promises softly glow.
They whisper words of light,
In the depths, we come to know.

Every flicker has a tale,
Of hopes that fill the air.
In their brilliance, we set sail,
Finding strength in what we share.

As constellations weave our fate,
We stand beneath their grace.
In each moment, we create,
A sacred, timeless space.

With every dawning light,
The stars remain inside.
Held within our hearts so bright,
In starlit dreams, we bide.

So gather 'neath that starry dome,
And cast your hopes up high.
In the universe, we roam,
Together, you and I.

The Symphony of Shared Moments

In the soft glow of evening light,
Laughter dances like birds in flight.
Echoes of joy weave through the air,
Every heartbeat sings a tune so rare.

Fingers entwined, our stories blend,
Every glance a silent send.
Time pauses for a fleeting chance,
In the rhythm of our shared dance.

Memories tucked in corners bright,
Candles flicker, casting soft light.
With each note, our spirits soar,
Together in this sweet rapport.

The world fades as we hum a song,
In this moment, we all belong.
A symphony crafted by hearts true,
Each note a thread, weaving me and you.

So let us savor this tender grace,
In the symphony, find our space.
With every moment, joy ignites,
Creating magic on starry nights.

Chronicles of the Heart

In pages worn, our tales unfold,
Whispers of love, stories bold.
Each chapter penned with tears and glee,
Crafting the saga of you and me.

Time carves lines upon our faces,
Marking journeys, sacred places.
With ink of dreams, we etch the past,
In these chronicles, our love will last.

Through valleys deep and mountains high,
Together we soar, reaching the sky.
Every heartbeat, a tale in disguise,
Reflecting the truth in each other's eyes.

Echoes of laughter, shadows of pain,
In this book, we dance in the rain.
Every page holds a heartbeat's song,
A testament to where we belong.

So here we write, with passion and fire,
In the chronicles, forever aspire.
For every moment, both near and far,
Is a verse in our love's memoir.

Unity in Diversity

In different hues, we find our grace,
Together we make a vibrant space.
With diverse voices, we weave a thread,
In the fabric of life, we are all led.

Cultures blend, like colors bright,
From dawn till dusk, we share the light.
In harmony, we walk side by side,
Celebrating the beauty in each stride.

Each story told, a world unveiled,
Through laughter and love, we have prevailed.
In unity, our strength does grow,
Like rivers merging, a ceaseless flow.

So let us dance in the rain of peace,
In every heartbeat, let love increase.
With open arms, we'll bridge the divide,
Embracing the beauty of our heart's pride.

Together we rise, hand in hand,
In this tapestry, forever we stand.
For in our hearts, we live the creed,
Unity blooms in every seed.

Moonlit Conversations

Beneath the stars, we softly speak,
In whispered tones, our souls we seek.
The moonlight bathes us in a glow,
Illuminating dreams we both know.

With every word, a secret shared,
In this stillness, our hearts are bared.
The world fades, and time stands still,
In this night, we find our will.

Gentle laughter, the night's embrace,
In each moment, we find our place.
The silver light dances on our skin,
In these conversations, love begins.

Stories drift like clouds above,
In the warmth of shared love.
With each gaze, new worlds we find,
In our moonlit realm, hearts intertwined.

So let us linger till the dawn,
In this hour, where dreams are drawn.
For every word, under the stars so bright,
Is a promise whispered in the night.

Heartfelt Echoes

In the silence of our hearts,
Whispers dance on gentle winds,
A symphony of dreams unfolds,
Binding us where love begins.

Through the tears and laughter shared,
Moments woven, tightly sewn,
Every echo tells a story,
Of a bond that's deeply grown.

In the shadows of the night,
Stars above begin to shine,
Their light reflects our journey,
Glowing softly, yours and mine.

Each heartbeat resonates hope,
A melody of trust and grace,
Together we can face the storms,
In love's warm, sweet embrace.

As we traverse this path of life,
Hand in hand, we boldly roam,
With each step, our spirits soar,
For in your heart, I find my home.

Radiance of Shared Smiles

A smile exchanged, a spark ignites,
Lighting paths in darkest nights,
In echoes bright, joy freely flows,
Creating warmth that gently glows.

Through whispered words and playful tease,
We find our rhythm, hearts at ease,
In laughter's dance, we take our flight,
Two souls united, pure delight.

With every gaze, intentions clear,
The beauty of friendship we hold dear,
In shared moments, life's magic shines,
Carving memories, like rarest wines.

With open hearts, we face each day,
Together in our unique way,
In the tapestry of time we weave,
Radiant bonds, we believe.

So here's to us, vibrant and free,
In the garden of smiles, you and me,
With each glance shared, a treasure found,
In the joy of connection, we are unbound.

Shadows of Companionship

In twilight's glow, we find our place,
Together, time begins to trace,
The shadows cast by dreams we share,
In each moment, love's gentle care.

Through winding paths, hand in hand,
We navigate this promised land,
In every challenge, side by side,
With courage found in eyes so wide.

When doubts arise, we stand our ground,
In the silence, strength is found,
In whispered fears and tender sighs,
We lift each other towards the skies.

For in the dark, true friends provide,
A light to guide us, our hearts' pride,
Through every trial and every ache,
Together, we will never break.

So let us wander, hearts entwined,
In shadows cast, true love defined,
In shared glances and unspoken vows,
We nurture life, here and now.

Stories Etched in Time

In pages worn, our tales unfold,
A chapter bright, a story bold,
Each moment lived, a line now scribed,
In the book of life, we've thrived.

With laughter's ink and sorrow's pen,
We paint a canvas, time and again,
Every setback, a lesson learned,
In the fire of love, our souls burned.

Through seasons' change, we find our way,
In daylight's sun and dusky gray,
Together, we chart the paths we know,
In dreams awakened, seeds we sow.

Memory's whispers call us near,
To cherished times we hold so dear,
In every story, a heartbeat flows,
In the essence of life, our love grows.

So turn the page, let's write anew,
In every word, a piece of you,
For in our tales, forever entwined,
Are stories etched in heart and mind.

The Art of Staying Close

In shadows deep, we find our light,
A whispered word, a gentle night.
With every laugh, with every sigh,
We weave our dreams, just you and I.

Through winding roads, our feet will tread,
In simple moments, love is fed.
With open hearts, we face the dawn,
A tapestry of life we're drawn.

The bond we share, a steady thread,
In storms and calm, by hope we're led.
Though time may change, our souls remain,
In artful ties, we bear no pain.

With patient hands, we build anew,
In every glance, an unspoken cue.
Through trials faced, hearts intertwined,
In the dance of trust, our love aligned.

Each step we take, a sacred chance,
In every silence, love's sweet dance.
In laughter shared and tears that flow,
We master well the art of close.

Timelines of Tenderness

In moments small, our history grows,
Soft murmurs shared, as time bestows.
The chapters woven, side by side,
In gentle ways, our hearts abide.

With every heartbeat, stories bloom,
In whispered dreams, we chase the loom.
Timeline etched, with care refined,
Tenderness in every line.

The pages turn, yet still we write,
Through seasons bold and starry nights.
Each scar a gem, each joy a light,
In the tapestry, our love takes flight.

From laughter's spark to sorrow's grace,
In life's embrace, we find our place.
In memories held, so close and dear,
Timelines of tenderness, crystal clear.

A journey shared, where hearts collide,
In every breath, we won't reside.
The future waits, with hands outstretched,
In love's sweet truth, our hearts are etched.

Footprints on the Path of Time

In soft-lit trails, our journey we trace,
With every step, we leave a grace.
In sands of moments, footprints lie,
A map of love beneath the sky.

Through fields of gold and shadows cast,
In echoes loud, our futures past.
Each footfall sings of stories told,
In gentle winds, our dreams unfold.

With courage strong, we brave the climb,
In every heartbeat, echoes time.
Through trials faced, we stand as one,
With every dusk, a brighter sun.

Beneath the stars, we walk with grace,
In every glance, each tight embrace.
The path we carve, a sacred rhyme,
As love leaves footprints on the time.

In whispered vows, we tread so near,
Through winding paths, there's naught to fear.
With hand in hand, we weave our fate,
On time's sweet canvas, we create.

The Rhythm of Familiar Hearts

In echoes soft, our hearts align,
A cadence found in love's design.
With every beat, the world will sway,
In rhythm sweet, we dance and play.

Through tender glances, fires ignite,
In silent moments, hearts take flight.
The melody of souls combined,
A symphony in every mind.

With every note, the past revives,
In harmony, our spirit thrives.
Through trials faced, we find the tune,
In every heart, a hopeful rune.

With whispered words, we craft a song,
In timeless beats, where we belong.
The rhythm flows with breath divine,
In familiar hearts, our souls entwine.

Through stormy nights and sunny days,
The pulse of love forever stays.
In simple joys, the music starts,
In perfect time, our familiar hearts.

Sunlit Paths and Moonlit Talks

Beneath the sky, where sunlight streams,
We wander through our gentle dreams.
Each path we take, a story writ,
In the warmth of day, we brightly sit.

As twilight falls, we share our thoughts,
In moonlit glow, where time forgot.
These talks of ours, like whispers soft,
In the night air, our hearts aloft.

With every step, the world feels wide,
Our spirits lift, our fears collide.
Together forged, through thick and thin,
A bond that grows, where love begins.

Through golden beams and silver light,
We find our way, from day to night.
Each path we tread, a dance anew,
In sunlit grace, in skies of blue.

In every laugh, in every sigh,
We weave the tale as time slips by.
With hearts aglow, we walk this way,
Sunlit paths and moonlit play.

The Endless Loop of Kindness

In a world where shadows creep,
A simple smile, the heart will keep.
With gentle words and open hands,
We sow the seeds in barren lands.

Each act of grace, a ripple spreads,
From one small deed, the heart is fed.
Like petals falling in the spring,
Kindness blooms, it's everything.

A listening ear, a shoulder there,
In times of need, we always care.
Through stormy seas or skies of blue,
Our circle grows, united, true.

Though days can be both dark and long,
A kind word shared makes spirits strong.
From random acts to gestures grand,
Together, we will take a stand.

The endless loop, it circles round,
With every heartbeat, love is found.
In this embrace, we find our place,
Forever bound in endless grace.

Verses of Enduring Companionship

Through storms and sun, we walk this road,
In every moment, our love bestowed.
With laughter shared, and sorrows faced,
In time's embrace, we find our pace.

In gentle whispers, our secrets flow,
As seasons change, our bond will grow.
Through trials and triumphs, side by side,
In life's great dance, we take our stride.

As stars align in evening's grace,
We carve our footprint, a sacred place.
In every heartbeat, a tale unfolds,
Of friendship deep and love untold.

With every year, our memories blend,
In every loss, in every mend.
Together we rise, together we fall,
In the symphony of life, we hear the call.

These verses penned with heart and soul,
In every chapter, we feel the whole.
With every glance, and every sigh,
Enduring love will never die.

The Saga of Us

In whispers soft, our story begins,
Two wanderers lost, seeking skin.
With every laugh, with every tear,
The saga of us draws ever near.

Through winding paths and restless nights,
We forged a bond, a spark that ignites.
From silent stares to endless chatter,
In each fleeting moment, love is what matters.

With hands entwined, we face the storms,
In darkest nights, our hearts keep warm.
Every chapter penned, with hopes and dreams,
Together we rise, or so it seems.

In twilight glow, our dreams unfold,
In every moment, a tale retold.
With passion bright, we chase the dawn,
In the saga of us, we carry on.

As pages turn and seasons change,
Through all the highs, the lows, the strange.
With unwavering love that never rusts,
We write the saga, forever, just us.

Laughter Through the Lens of Time

In shadows cast by days gone by,
Echoes of joy bring forth a sigh.
Memories dance in the soft moonlight,
Laughter weaves through the fabric of night.

A snapshot caught in a fleeting glance,
Captures a moment, a fleeting chance.
With every smile, a story unfolds,
Time stands still as the heart retolds.

Each giggle threads through history's seam,
A whisper of joy, a sweet, tender dream.
Through ages past, a melody rings,
Laughter, a gift that true friendship brings.

We gather the echoes, let the past flow,
Painting our lives in a radiant glow.
In laughter, both timeless and new,
A bridge we build, as if crafted by glue.

So let us cherish the moments we share,
With laughter as our compass, anywhere.
Through lenses of time, we'll always find,
The joy in our hearts—a bond so kind.

The Ties That Bind

In silent whispers, the truth unfolds,
Threads of connection in stories told.
From heart to heart, an invisible thread,
Ties us together, where love is spread.

In laughter and tears, we walk side by side,
Through every challenge, our spirits abide.
In shadows and light, we find our way,
With bonds unbroken, come what may.

Each moment shared, a treasure we crave,
In the tapestry woven, we're brave.
For friendships like roots still bloom in the ground,
In the garden of souls, our strength can be found.

Through storms and seasons, we rise and we fall,
The ties that bind, they weave through it all.
A network of love that time can't erase,
In every embrace, we all find our place.

So cherish the ties, the bonds that don't fade,
In silence or laughter, our love is displayed.
With each heartbeat, our spirits entwine,
For it's love that we hold, the true ties that bind.

Ancestral Affection

In stories whispered, roots intertwine,
Echoes of love through the passage of time.
With every heartbeat, we feel their embrace,
Ancestral affection, a warm, sacred space.

Their dreams sail through us like rivers of light,
Guiding our paths in the dark of the night.
In laughter and tears, their spirits reside,
A legacy lived, with history as guide.

Through family gatherings, the bonds are sustained,
In dance and in song, affection maintained.
With every story, their essence is near,
Ancestral affection, a treasure held dear.

In whispers of wind, we hear their refrain,
Carriers of love, through joy and through pain.
Through every challenge, their wisdom we seek,
In the shadows of time, our roots are unique.

So let us honor the lineage we share,
With gratitude woven in threads of our care.
Ancestral affection, a bond we receive,
In the heart of our being, forever we believe.

Heartbeats in Harmony

In rhythms of life, our hearts beat as one,
In concert we flourish, like flowers in sun.
With every pulse, a melody rings,
Heartbeats in harmony, the joy that it brings.

In silence and laughter, our souls intertwine,
Creating a symphony that feels so divine.
With every glance, a note softly played,
In the dance of our hearts, love won't ever fade.

Through valleys and peaks, our journey unfolds,
Each moment a story, each memory gold.
With every heartbeat, a promise we make,
In the chorus of life, together we'll wake.

So let us embrace this beautiful song,
A rhythm of love that can't steer us wrong.
With heartbeats in harmony, we shall soar high,
A duet forever, beneath the vast sky.

In the windows of time, our music remains,
In whispers and shouts, our love still sustains.
With every heartbeat, our spirits align,
A resonance deep, eternal and fine.

Threads of Companionship

In laughter's echo, we find our way,
Two hearts entwined, come what may.
Through quiet nights and sunlight's smile,
Together we journey, mile by mile.

Through whispers soft, our secrets shared,
In every moment, knowing we cared.
Hand in hand, in storms we dance,
Embracing life, a cherished chance.

Through days of joy, through nights of tears,
Building memories across the years.
A tapestry woven, rich and bright,
In threads of love, our hearts take flight.

In silent gazes, our stories unfold,
In the warmth of touch, our lives retold.
Forever bound, in joy we stand,
In this journey, side by side, hand in hand.

With every chapter, our bond will grow,
In the garden of friendship, love we sow.
Through time and space, our spirits blend,
In this life's dance, there's no end.

The Garden of Shared Moments

In a garden where memories bloom,
We gather joy, dispelling gloom.
Every petal tells a tale,
Of laughter, love, and dreams that sail.

Beneath the sun, we weave the day,
In whispered hopes, we find our way.
With every breeze, our spirits soar,
In shared moments, we long for more.

The flowers dance in vibrant hues,
Reflecting laughter, and chosen views.
In softest grass, we lay at ease,
Time stands still, a gentle breeze.

With roots entwined, we stand as one,
Through every season, our bond is spun.
In twilight's glow, the shadows play,
In our garden, forever stay.

With every bloom, a promise made,
In this sacred ground, our love is laid.
Through years that pass, our hearts will thrive,
In the garden of moments, we come alive.

Affection's Journey

With every step, our path is bright,
Together we chase the fading light.
In whispers soft, our dreams arise,
Through winding roads, under painted skies.

A hand to hold, a heart to cheer,
In every smile, you draw me near.
Through valleys deep, up mountains high,
In affection's journey, we dare to fly.

We celebrate the little things,
The joy each friendship truly brings.
In every hug, a story shared,
In quiet moments, we've always cared.

Through tears and laughter, life unfolds,
In every memory, a tale retold.
With courage found in each embrace,
In affection's journey, we leave our trace.

As time moves on, our hearts will stay,
Side by side, come what may.
In love's embrace, we thrive and grow,
In every heartbeat, our connection glows.

Sunsets Shared

As the day fades, colors ignite,
We watch the sky turn gold and bright.
With every sunset, a dream takes flight,
In silent moments, hearts feel light.

Beneath the canvas of evening's glow,
In whispers shared, our spirits flow.
With fingers brushed, and laughter shared,
In the glow of dusk, we feel prepared.

The sun dips low, casting shadows long,
In twilight's hush, we sing our song.
With every glance, the world feels vast,
In these sunsets shared, memories cast.

We chase the dusk, where dreams align,
In fading light, our hearts entwine.
Through every hue that paints the skies,
In sunsets shared, our love never dies.

As stars awake and night draws near,
In the warm embrace, our loved ones cheer.
In every sunset, our stories blend,
In this journey of light, we transcend.

Unfolding Stories of Us

In whispers soft, we shared our dreams,
Under moonlight's watchful beams.
A tapestry of laughter spun,
Two souls entwined, now just begun.

In every glance, a tale unfolds,
In silent nods, our history holds.
Step by step through shadowed halls,
Echoes linger, as twilight calls.

Faded pages, yet love remains,
In the heart, where memory gains.
Every truth wrapped in a sigh,
Forever ours, as days pass by.

Through time's embrace, our voices blend,
In every curve, around each bend.
With every thread, our story grows,
In the silence, our spirit flows.

Together we weave, bright and bold,
In every chapter, warmth to hold.
As twilight gathers, tales ignite,
Unfolding stories in the night.

The Pulse of Shared Memories

Beneath the stars, a heartbeat thrums,
In laughter's echo, joy becomes.
A dance of dreams, both near and far,
Guided gently by a single star.

In fleeting moments, time will freeze,
Captured whispers in the breeze.
With every glance, a spark ignites,
In shadows deep, our love delights.

The pulse of days we hold so dear,
In every heartbeat, you are near.
With treasured thoughts, we journey on,
Through the night until the dawn.

In quiet rooms where silence speaks,
It's in our hearts that truth reveals.
A language strong, a bond so true,
In every memory, I find you.

From dawn to dusk, our spirits blend,
In all the moments, love transcends.
With every breath, a promise stays,
In shared memories, our love plays.

Parables of the Heart

In whispered tales of days gone by,
The heart reveals, beneath the sky.
Each lesson learned, a gentle guide,
In the journey where hopes abide.

Unraveled threads of joy and pain,
In every storm, love will remain.
With open eyes, we seek the light,
In parables shared, hearts take flight.

Through trials faced and bridges crossed,
In every gain, there's something lost.
Yet in the shadows, truth is found,
The heart speaks volumes, profound sound.

As seasons change and rivers flow,
Our stories weave, endlessly grow.
With wisdom gained from every heart,
In life's great book, we play our part.

With every word, we learn and teach,
In love's embrace, we seek to reach.
Parables of the heart will stay,
A timeless bond, come what may.

Melodies of the Past

In echoes soft of yesterday,
Where memories dance, they find their way.
A symphony of laughter sings,
With every note, the past still clings.

In fading light, old songs resound,
Reminders sweet that love is found.
In every chord, a heartbeat lies,
Embracing moments, sweet goodbyes.

With every tune, the spirit flies,
In gentle rhymes, our history ties.
Like autumn leaves that softly fall,
The melodies echo, through it all.

As twilight falls, the music plays,
A haunting tune of yesterdays.
In every sigh, a flicker glows,
A harmony that softly flows.

Together we sing, through joy and strife,
Melodies of the past, our life.
In every heart, a song will last,
As we embrace the love amassed.

Weaving Moments

In the quiet hours, we find our thread,
Stitching laughter, love, and dreams unsaid.
Each heartbeat echoes, a gentle chime,
Crafting memories, lost in time.

Sunset whispers, painting skies so bright,
Fingers entwined, we dance in twilight.
Every glance a note in our shared song,
Together we weave, where we belong.

The loom of life spins joy and strife,
Each woven moment, a precious life.
In tangled threads, the stories hide,
Unraveling softly, side by side.

As seasons shift, our tapestry grows,
In the warmth of love, the fabric glows.
With every stitch, a promise we make,
In this grand design, there's nothing at stake.

Let's weave forever, through day and night,
In every shadow, we find our light.
Moments entwined, in colors so bold,
A glorious tapestry, our hearts unfold.

The Language of Touch

A whisper of skin, electric and warm,
In every caress, a place to disarm.
Fingers that dance like leaves in the air,
A silent story, embracing our care.

In the brush of a hand, worlds intertwine,
Conversations spoken without a sign.
Every gentle squeeze, a promise clear,
In the language of touch, love draws near.

Eyes that close, as souls intertwine,
In this tender moment, you are mine.
The warmth of your breath, I long to feel,
In this soft silence, our hearts reveal.

Time stands still in a lover's embrace,
Lost in the magic of your sweet grace.
Each heartbeat a rhythm, a soft serenade,
In the dance of our fingers, love won't fade.

Let us explore the depths of this art,
In every touch, we craft from the heart.
With each gentle moment, we rise and we fall,
In the language of touch, we have it all.

Timeless Odyssey

Through the waves of ages, we sail away,
In the arms of the stars, we find our way.
Each sunset a chapter, each dawn a new page,
In this timeless odyssey, we break out of the cage.

Mountains may tremble, the rivers may shift,
But in our hearts, love remains a gift.
As we roam the galaxies, hand in hand,
In the dance of forever, we make our stand.

With dreams like constellations in the night,
We wander through shadows, chasing the light.
Every moment's a treasure, every laugh a song,
In this ancient journey, we both belong.

Under the moon's gaze, we find our breath,
In the echo of time, love conquers death.
Through the eons we travel, forever free,
Bound by our spirits, just you and me.

So let our hearts wander, with no end in sight,
In this timeless odyssey, we take flight.
With each shared heartbeat, a cosmos we weave,
In the fabric of being, together we believe.

Chronicles of Together

In the book of us, the pages unfold,
Stories of laughter, both daring and bold.
Through whispers and glances, our chapters create,
A tale of two souls, through love and fate.

From the first moment, a spark ignites,
In the heart of the night, we bask in delights.
With every heartbeat, the story takes flight,
In the chronicles of together, everything feels right.

The pages may tear, but our bond stays strong,
In the rhythm of life, we both belong.
Every twist and turn, a lesson we learn,
In the fires of love, every passion will burn.

With the ink of our tears, we write every line,
In the journey of us, our hearts intertwine.
As seasons change, and years roll by,
In the chronicles of together, love will never die.

So let's finish this tale of love ever true,
With every page turned, there's always me and you.
In this beautiful saga, forever we'll stay,
In the chronicles of together, come what may.

The Beat of Shared Hearts

In the quiet of a crowded room,
Two souls whisper secrets, bloom.
A glance exchanged, a spark ignites,
The rhythm of love, casting lights.

Heartbeat synchronizes, soft and clear,
With every pulse, they draw near.
In perfect harmony, they sway,
A dance of souls, come what may.

Every laugh sings like a song,
In this symphony, they belong.
Through shadows dark and sunlit days,
Their love, a melody that stays.

Hand in hand, they walk the line,
Two hearts, one beat, truly divine.
Through trials faced and joys embraced,
In this duet, they find their place.

Forever echoing, their vow set,
In the meadows of dreams, no regret.
The beat of shared hearts forever binds,
A timeless tune that love finds.

Serendipitous Encounters

In the bustling streets of fate and chance,
Two strangers meet, their eyes in a trance.
An unexpected smile, a moment shared,
Two wandering souls, unprepared.

Paths crossed briefly, yet time stands still,
An unspoken bond, a mutual thrill.
Laughter spills with stories untold,
In that instant, a connection unfolds.

In a café, under starlit skies,
They weave their dreams, they vocalize.
With each word, the world fades away,
In the magic of now, they choose to stay.

Cadence of voices that linger on,
In serendipity, love is born.
Moments cherished, new paths to devise,
In the dance of chance, they realize.

With memories forged, they part their ways,
Yet echoes remain, like sun-kissed rays.
A chance encounter, a timeless spark,
In the book of life, they've left their mark.

Ageless Affection

In the whispers of time, love stays bright,
Through seasons of change, a guiding light.
Hands that have weathered life's cruel storms,
In ageless affection, the heart warms.

Through laughter shared and tears that flowed,
In every moment, their love glowed.
Like a fine wine, aged to perfection,
Their bond, a treasure, hearts in connection.

Stars may dim, yet they'll never fade,
In the tapestry of life, love's serenade.
Through gray skies and sunny days,
Together they journeyed through love's maze.

In quiet corners, memories entwine,
A legacy built, purely divine.
In every wrinkle, every line drawn,
Ageless affection, forever strong.

In the twilight, hand in hand they'll stand,
Two hearts together, a timeless strand.
In the echoes of love, they'll find their way,
In the ageless embrace of yesterday.

Galaxy of Us

In the cosmos of dreams, we collide,
Stars aligning, a love we're proud to abide.
Each moment glimmers, planets in dance,
In this galaxy of us, we take a chance.

Nebulas swirl with the colors we paint,
Our laughter, a melody sweet, never faint.
In the vastness of space, we carve our place,
Two souls entwined in an endless embrace.

Constellations guide as we drift and soar,
With every heartbeat, we crave more.
Through black holes and comets, we navigate,
In our orbit, love will never wait.

So let the stars watch with glistening eyes,
As we chase infinity beneath the skies.
With every spark and glowing dust,
In this galaxy of us, we trust.

From dawn till dusk, through cosmic nights,
We paint our love in celestial lights.
In the universe built from our dreams,
Forever entwined, nothing's as it seems.

Hearts Entwined Through Time

In the depths of night, we find our way,
Two souls connected, come what may.
Through laughter and tears, we softly glide,
In the dance of life, forever side by side.

Threads of fate weave a tapestry bright,
Every whispered word, a flickering light.
Across the ages, our hearts do soar,
In the endless embrace that we both adore.

Moments cherished, in the heart they stay,
Glistening memories, never fade away.
In the echo of laughter, we shines anew,
Hand in hand, forever, just me and you.

In the silence shared, we hear the song,
Of timeless love, where we both belong.
Through the sands of time, we walk as one,
Hearts entwined, our journey's just begun.

In every heartbeat, a promise we keep,
In the quiet night, our secrets seep.
Together we'll blossom, together we'll grow,
In the garden of time, our love will flow.

Shared Secrets of the Soul

Beneath the stars, we whisper low,
Secrets hidden, only we know.
In the quiet night, our dreams take flight,
Two souls entwined, shining so bright.

In the shadows cast by the moon's soft glow,
We share our hopes, let the feelings flow.
With every glance, a deeper glance returned,
In the warmth of silence, our hearts have burned.

Through winding paths, our journeys combine,
In the fabric of fate, your heart's in mine.
We laugh and we cry, in harmony sweet,
In the dance of our souls, we're ever complete.

In the embrace of night, we find our peace,
In the echo of love, all worries cease.
Each secret we share, a thread in the seam,
Woven together, the fabric of dreams.

Time may stretch, but our bond will stay,
In the sacred space where we both lay.
Guardians of secrets, we'll ever remain,
Two restless hearts, forever unchained.

Memories in the Moonlight

Under the moon's soft, silvery gleam,
We wander through nights woven from dreams.
With every step, memories flash bright,
In the gentle caress of the warm night light.

By the babbling brook, we pause and reflect,
On moments we shared, love's sweet effect.
Each whisper of wind carries a tune,
Of laughter and joy, beneath the moon.

In the canvas of night, our story unfolds,
With colors of love that never grow old.
We chase down the stars, with hopes in our hearts,
In the rhythm of night, our adventure starts.

When shadows dance and the world fades away,
Our spirits ignite in the cool night sway.
Forever enshrined in the silence we keep,
Each heartbeat like secrets, ours to reap.

In the pale dawn, we'll greet the new day,
But in the moonlight, our dreams stay at play.
For memories linger, persist and entwine,
In the glow of sweet night, your heart stays with mine.

Kindred Spirits, Forever

In the forest deep, where shadows play,
We roam together, come what may.
With laughter that echoes through the trees,
Two kindred spirits, dancing in the breeze.

Amidst the wildflowers, we pause and share,
In every moment, a bond so rare.
Through the trials faced, love's light will shine,
In the tapestry woven, your heart's in mine.

With every sunrise, new adventures await,
Hand in hand, we challenge fate.
In the symphony of life, we find our song,
Together we flourish, where we belong.

As seasons change, our love shall grow,
With roots entwined, through ebb and flow.
In the dance of time, we'll always stay,
Kindred spirits, come what may.

In the twilight hours, when the world is still,
We'll cherish each moment, and hearts will thrill.
Forever together, steadfast and true,
In the story of love, it's me and you.

Milton Keynes UK
Ingram Content Group UK Ltd.
UKHW022110061124
450854UK00006B/69

9 789916 867280